Ethnographic Terminalia: Philadelphia 2009
Crane Arts

Published by the Society for Visual Anthropology, a section of the
American Anthropological Association. 2300 Clarendon Blvd.,
Suite 1301. Arlington, VA 22201

The review essay in this volume was originally published in the journal
Visual Anthropology Review. Our grateful acknowledgement to
the editors.

Edited by Ethnographic Terminalia:
Craig Campbell, Kate Hennessy, Fiona P. McDonald, Trudi Lynn Smith,
Stephanie Takaragawa

Lead editors and print design: Kate Hennessy and Rachel Topham

Exhibition Photography: Ethnographic Terminalia

Cover Design: Ethnographic Terminalia, Rachel Topham and
Ian Kirkpatrick

ISBN 978-1-931303-47-7

Philidelphia 2009:

Contributors

Ethnographic Terminalia
Philadelphia 2009

Crane Arts

2009 Curators
Craig Campbell
Anabelle Rodriguez
Fiona P. McDonald

Organizational Team
Kate Hennessy
Stephanie Takaragawa

General installation view, Philadelphia, 2009.

Acknowledgements

The support of many individuals and groups was essential to the realization of Ethnographic Terminalia. Our local partner and guest curator Anabelle Rodriguez played a central role in all stages of the exhibition. Her enthusiasm and generosity were crucial for success in this inaugural year. Crane Arts is a remarkable institution and we are indebted to them for generously entrusting their formidable space to us.

Thank you to the Crane community and especially to Jamie and Nicholas for all of their coordinating assistance. Temple University provided on the ground support for the exhibition at the Ice Box Gallery in Crane Arts. Thank you to the volunteers whose commitment of time and energy was important to the success of the exhibition: Kimberly Dukes, Nicole Welk, Ana Vizcarra, Olive Sheehan, Heather Pellecchia, Megan Gibes, Eunice Yu, Courtney Waltimye, Anna Humphries, Keith Marchiafava.

Support was also provided by The Society for Visual Anthropology, The Americo Paredes Center for Cultural Studies (University of Texas at Austin), Workshop for Intermedia Ethnographies, Chris Fletcher (University of Alberta), Mike Evans (Community, Culture and Global Studies at University of British Columbia, Okanagan), and the Graduate School at University College London.

Thank you to Stella Artois (Sarah Razionale, of Anheuser-Busch) and Oyster Bay Wines (John Freeman, Australia) who sponsored the opening.

Finally, we would like to express our sincere appreciation to all of the artists who participated in Ethnographic Terminalia.

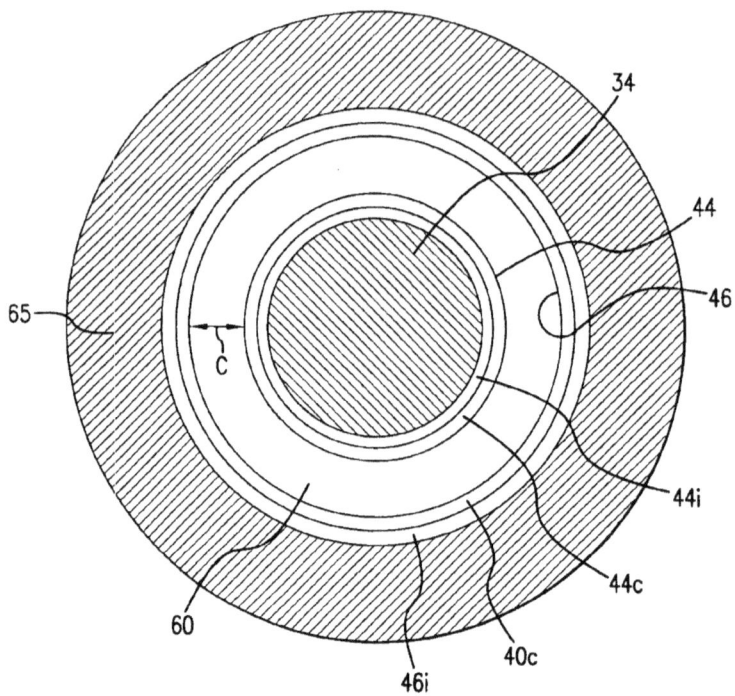

34

44

46

65

C

44i

44c

40c

60

46i

Ethnographic Terminialia

The terminus is the end, the boundary, and the border. It is also a beginning, its own place, a site of experience and encounter. *Ethnographic Terminalia* exhibits new forms of anthropology engaged with contemporary art practice. Playfully exploring reflexivity and positionality, we ask what lies within and what lies beyond disciplinary territories. No longer content to subordinate the sensorium to theoretical and expository monographs, *Ethnographic Terminalia* is a curatorial collective motivated by possibilities of new media, locations, and methods.

General installation view, Philadelphia, 2009.

General installation view, Philadelphia, 2009.

General installation view, Philadelphia, 2009.

General installation view, Philadelphia, 2009.

Trudi Lynn Smith

Portable Camera Obscura: a quest

The installation *Portable Camera Obscura* is a walk-in, room-sized camera. A temporary architecture, it is a lightproof tent environment that projects an image of the outside view onto the walls of the tent with a simple lens. The image that projects into the tent is unfixed and only experienced by those who bear witness at that moment.

First positioned in the location of popular photographic views in Waterton Lakes National Park, Alberta, in summer 2009, participants were able to enter the tent to see the landscape projected onto the wall of the structure. Tracking historical photographs, the camera was installed in several popular locations for image-making in the park. I also mounted an expedition style journey into the back-country of Waterton. I invited community members that 'speak for nature' (wardens, ecologists, environmentalists, environmental educators) to attempt to re-locate an historical photograph. With me as the guide, we went on a quest to investigate historical photographs, to experiment with the distance between representation and represented, and to play with what a more ethically and ecologically sound relationship between image and place might look like. We took the archive out for a walk as a way to transform the historical photograph from a document (or monument) back into a located, community act. The tent was an experiential foundation for communication.

A collaborative space and an architecture of attention, the installation was built for loitering, conversations, and looking differently at a view and at a photographic act. This work focuses on active and dynamic experiences as catalysts for generating communicative processes that can spark new knowledge about nature and representation in Canada.`

In the gallery space, *Portable Camera Obscura* forms a part of a larger project of gallery works that I install as social work-spaces to investigate archival photographs. One step removed from the site of production, and one more level of mediation, inside the Portable Camera Obscura the viewer sees a 50 x 72 cm hand tinted mid twentieth century photograph illuminated, "Waterton Lake from the Prince of Wales Hotel in Canada" taken in mid 20th century by the photographer Kabel, an employee of Great Northern Rail.

Erica Lehrer & Hannah Smotrich

Jewish? Heritage? In Poland?

In post-Holocaust, post-Communist Poland — home now to only a tiny minority of Jews — new representations of Poland's "Jewish heritage" abound. Especially prevalent in tourist zones, these manifestations are understood, and judged, very differently by local Poles, local Jews, and visitors from abroad.

If one single image is a lightening rod for the many questions raised by these new displays of Jewishness, it is the figure of the Jew itself. Caught in a web of overlapping visual histories, the image of the Jew is informed by many precedents: Marc Chagall's flying rabbis, Roman Vishniac's impoverished Hasidim, and Hollywood's *Fiddler on the Roof* on the one hand and anti-Semitic stereotypes, perfected in Nazi propaganda, on the other.

These representations raise questions:
> • of ownership: Can a non-Jew produce Judaica?
> • of context: Similar images in Israel or New York arouse no comment.
> • of intent: Are these representations memorial, mercenary, talismanic?
> • On what basis do we deem these images "Okay" or "Not Okay"? You decide. (And tell us why.)

This piece is one sketch in an ongoing investigation of how one might curate ethnography in ways that capture some of the theoretical advances of the post-Writing Culture era: attention to multiple perspectives, assertions of authority, self-reflection, dialogue, global flows, and above all representational experimentation. It grows out of an essay I wrote about the evolving trade in Jewish figurines in Poland (*Repopulating Jewish Poland – in Wood*, Polin 2003). I wanted to see if it was possible to translate into installation form the core argument:

that even a hot-button item that many view as "kitsch" (at best) is suspended in a web of international transcultural memorial exchanges in which many of us are implicated. And if this works, perhaps other areas of historical conflict may be curated in ways that create openings for dialogue as well.

The broader experiment is to look at ethnographic data for key social and cultural issues, questions, and problems, and distill these into exhibitable units. Because significant sites, symbols, utterances and gestures communicate on multiple levels and mean different things to different people, a central goal is to find ways make dialogue integral to the exhibit. The aim is to reframe common sights, sounds, and experiences in ways that create new engagement and fresh understanding.

Kate Hennessy and Oliver Neumann

Media on the City – The Lee Building

Media on the City – The Lee Building is a video projection that documents the dismantling of a billboard and its steel substructure on the top of Vancouver's landmarked Lee Building over a period of four months. Constructed in 1912, the Lee Building is known as Vancouver's first "skyscraper," and still stands out prominently against the downtown skyline. The billboard was erected in the 1950s, and is commonly assumed to interfere with the view of Vancouver's downtown and mountains from residential buildings recently constructed in the area. The recent deconstruction of the advertising sign follows the loss of a decade-long court battle by the building's residents and owners that contested the city's 1970-era ban on billboards in the city. The removal of the sign is a manifestation of two parallel but also contradicting ideologies shaping the city: new urban living and developments versus the preservation of existing inner-city neighborhoods and buildings and their embeddedness into the existing urban fabric. In a city that draws heavily on its surrounding landscape, the transformation of the Lee Building raises questions regarding the scales of reference central to urban life, playing with tensions between active neighborhoods and the commodified city with its focus on the visual.

Observing the demolition of the building's advertising panels, *Media on the City – The Lee Building* positions the rapid transformation of the city against the recurring everyday experience of the city dweller. A singular view of an instance of urban architecture illustrates the ongoing negotiation of shifting ideologies of the urban in a rapidly developing young North American city. The video documentation takes the presence of the building as a constant; shifting light and weather conditions through changing seasons document and reposition the building in its urban and landscape surroundings. References to foreground, middleground, and background are constantly redefined. At the same time, the video positions the viewer as an active participant in the negotiations of spatial references. Changing weather and lighting dynamically alter the visual field and reconstitute the experience of the urban context.

This ongoing re-setting of the architecture highlights the contradictory ideologies at play in Vancouver that ultimately tie urban culture to notions of scale. Rather than an obstruction of the view of Vancouver's downtown skyline in its natural setting with the Pacific Coast Mountains beyond, the owners and residents of the Lee Building see the advertising panel and the related income as a contribution to the local community. Proceeds from the advertising helped finance the building's residential and commercial units and made spaces affordable for local artists and community initiatives. The city, to the contrary, views Vancouver's natural setting as a central part of its experience, and any obstruction of the view that threatens to disconnect the city from its landscape background is seen to undermine the city's character and needs to be removed.

Gordana Zivkovic and Marko Zivkovic
Lovable Edmonton

"There is something magic and electric in the simple fact of choosing a subject (a place, a moment, an event, a person, things, stones, trees) and working around them, into them, picture by picture. Is it an illusion, or am I right to feel that you have only really seen something when you have fully, lovingly, sensually photographed it?" Thus spoke Fosco Maraini a photographer and ethnographer extraordinaire.
Marko makes painstaking photographic studies of empty bus stops on the route of the Bus No. 6 in Edmonton using medium and large format cameras, B&W film, and enlarging to vintage graded paper in the darkroom. Gordana colors the photos in the old coloring technique.

As recent immigrants to Canada, Gordana and Marko are trying to make the city of Edmonton their own by lovingly documenting bus stops as those urban nodes that tend to be relegated to the realm of the "infra-ordinary" – too commonplace to be noticed. This kind of prolonged, sustained, obsessive attention to detail sharpens perception and lifts the infra-ordinary into the extra-ordinary. It is ethnographic in its embrace of the Malinowskian "imponderabilia of everyday life," and artistic in its concern with form and emotion. The inspiration for this project comes from George Perec's *Species of Spaces*, Hiroshige's *53 Stages of Tokaido*, and Martin Parr's *Boring Postcards*.

Christopher Fletcher

The Sound of Le Corbusier's Paris

"Architecture is a confrontation with our own senses"
(Libeskind 2009)

Sounds "carry their spaces with them – they are space bearers"
(Smalley 2007:38)

This sound installation is an outcome of anthropological research on the imbrications of space, the senses and the built environment. The ambient sounds of several Parisian buildings designed by renowned modernist architect Le Corbusier are presented through specially designed speakers. Exteriors and, where possible, interior sounds were collected for all of Le Corbusier's Paris oeuvre. An experiment in acousmatic ethnography, it is hoped that experiencing the sonic environment of these places will encourage consideration the auditory in relation to the other senses when encountering places generally. The project is part of a longstanding interest in space as a personal, social, and cultural project. Who we are is where we are would be one way to situate this dynamic.

This installation is also enlivened by the anthropology of the senses through which we can see that broad cultural orientations are sensually specific and that these vary over time and locale. In our visually oriented cultural worlds what do we make of sound? In particular what role does the incidental, ambient, non-specific sound in which we are always immersed have in shaping our understanding of place and ourselves? As I write this it is nearly 11PM and there are increasingly strident construction noises growing from the east side of my hotel room. They emanate from somewhere in this complex of buildings that includes my room. It appears to get louder as the time I would like to sleep comes closer. We habituate to sounds or irritate to them. The visual is different – we close our eyes and it's gone. Not so with sound. The sounds in this installation are meant to challenge the listener to interrogate their movements through space; to refigure the place of the auditory within the sensory realm of the everyday.

There is nothing to see here, or almost nothing. I shy away from representing the sites opting instead to replay them. What does listening bring us that seeing doesn't? At the very least it disorients us to place, complicating our ability to know it, and repositions the listener as needing to decode the where-are-we which otherwise flows so easily from vision. Some of the sites feature bird sounds, footfalls of pedestrians, elements of conversations that fade in and out as people walk by. Others are more cacophonous, with traffic, banging and buzzing occupying the aural space. Even in an exclusively acoustic experience we will attempt to "see" the building in the imaginative work that follows the listening. We lack an appropriate language for the aural, substituting one sense for the other. Aural space is in need of en-tuning rather than en-visioning.

Roderick Coover

Unknownterritories and **The Harvest**

Unknownterritories

The traveler transforms perceptions into narratives and places into imagined spaces — spaces in which the traveler grasps both a sense of the temporal moment and imagines the potential trajectories that the events of any moment might hold. When John Wesley Powell navigated the Colorado River in 1869 and began a project of mapping the western deserts, he envisioned what the desert landscape might look like populated with settlers. He argued for sustainable growth and was expelled from office. About 100 years later, writer Edward Abbey encounters a very different West. The land is owned, mapped, gridded, dammed, mined, and crisscrossed with roads, paths and pipelines. The writer walks the canyons to re-imagine a desert landscape. He draws attention to the destruction of the land including the construction of dams that flooded and buried the natural and cultural sites John Wesley Powell once wrote about. His works give record to a 1960s and 1970s culture of desert environmental activism and rebellion. Viewers explore the processes that led Abbey and his local community to make the choices they did — choices grounded in an American tradition that goes back to the Boson Tea party: direct action and sabotage. These new works have been featured in galleries and online venues. An online discussion will be held Sunday at 1030am in conjunction with an exhibition funded by Subito (www.subitopress.org).

For more information about unknown territories, visit the project: www.unknownterritories.org.

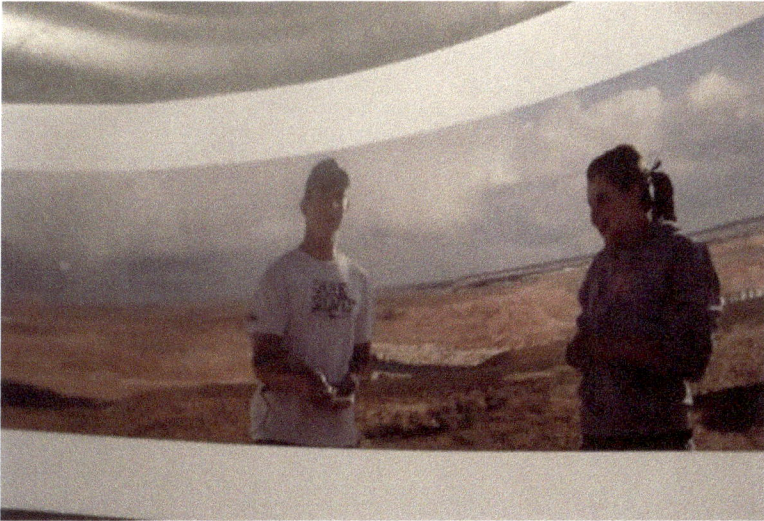

The Harvest

The Harvest is a photographic study of the Burgundian vendange recorded in the village of Bouzeron in the Cote Chalonaise. The installation employs four bands of images and text each using differing compositional forms to incorporate various stages of production and representation in a finished work. This series and the related film, *The Language of Wine*, explore how the terminology of a metier can serve as metaphors in the individual expression of personal views and goals.

The work was supported with funding from the Chicago Group On Modern France and elsewhere and the film has been featured in electronic media arts exhibitions and film festivals such as Documenta Madrid. Elements of this work are published in the CD-ROM Cultures In Webs: Working in Hypermedia With The Documentary Image (Eastgate.com) and as the DVD, *The Language Of Wine* (www.Languageofwine.com).

Jayasinhji Jhala
Rann Walk Ocean and **Breathings**

Rann Walk Ocean

Rann Walk Ocean is one example of an ongoing series of video paintings by Bapa and Liluye Jhala. The VPs are anchored in the idea of the magical mundane. Particular, daily, seasonal, cyclical, episodic, and millennial events occur in all ecologies and environments. All living things domesticate them even as they impregnate them. More importantly, they celebrate them. These environments are mirrored in the habits and patterns of the imagined possible: between species and between humans. The magical mundane is a phrase for the normal that offers surprise to the alien.

An ethno-surreal response evokes experience through memory of the fragment, of immensity through the momentary. The quirky, improbable, unexpected imagined. It suggests relationships and interdependence without demonstration. Communication occurs through transduction, by travel along tangents, and is palpable if it resonates with the viewer. Explanation is not attempted, suggestion births inquiry.

Breathings

Trained as a gemologist, filmmaker, and anthropologist Bapa Jhala assembles a mobile sculpture called 'Breathings' that are composed of feathers, quills, shells, seeds, gemstones, and other organic and found materials. The mobility and velocity comes from air volumes being moved by the moments of persons in confined spaces. Longevity of motion is sustained by the continuum of gravity. Movement makes the invisible visible. The association of obits and stillness with meditative practices confers the idea that dynamic action resides in perceived inaction.

Craig Campbell

Mobile Agitational Cinema: Iteration no. 1

Through the 1920s and 30s a corps of dedicated communist agitators travelled through remote regions of Siberia. One of the most significant cultural interventions they produced was the mobile cinema. Setting up their projectors in tents, shacks, and cabins they threw the shimmering images of distant scenes and foreign stories into the taiga landscape.

Mobile cinemas were one of a host of technological interventions in the lives of indigenous Siberians prior to the construction of permanent cultural facilities and the forced sedentarization of nomadic hunters and reindeer herders. Along with Western medicine, the cinematic apparatus introduced a powerful and persuasive new way of being and imagining that reinforced otherness but simultaneously helped to interpolate indigenous peoples into an internationalist and inclusive project of radical cultural transformation.

Mobile Agitational Cinema: Iteration no. 1 is a purpose-built mobile cinema; a large canvas expedition tent. The moving pictures in this iteration are not meant to agitate for revolution but to intimate unfamiliar and distant worlds. The mobile cinema plays on the ethnographer's dream world as well as his role as cultural interpreter. It transmits images of the taiga: emanations of ficto-documents and implied histories.

IMAGES
The British Library Endangered Archives Project, Mihaly Hoppal, Anatoly Martynov, Thomas Ross Miller, Craig Campbell, Aaron Munson, Hiroki Takakura, Reiss-Engelhorns Museen, American Museum of Natural History

SOUNDS

Shaman songs: Thomas Ross Miller, American Museum of Natural History, Indiana University Archives of Traditional Music, Pushkin National Library (Yakutsk) Musicians: Athanasy Fyodorov, N.M. Likhachev, "Ma'shka," Eduard Noxorov, Ivan Tretyakov, N.T. Zakharov Sea Ice: Robert Asher, Glaciological Institute Reindeer: Pulse of the Planet Wolves: Sittelle Wind, Fire, Birds: John Hudak
www.lindenmuseum.de
www.youtube.com/user/anthroart

Maryam Kashani

"Interview: Nasser 10/23/02"

Interview: Nasser 10/23/02 is an oral history interview conducted for a feature length documentary, *Best in the West* (2006). The installation reflects on the interview, which given enough time and perhaps direction, can traverse great emotional and gestured terrain. In the telling of one's own life, whether it be a joyous moment of discovery or a tragic account of death or regret, one's body will either open itself up to memory or bolt down the doors. Whether it is the presence of a camera, a captivated audience, or the time and space to explore one's story in detail, or a combination of the above, something happens in an oral interview. And with filming, it is not only audible, but visible. It becomes a record, not necessarily of a particular event in or span of history, but the telling of a history, filtered through perspective, memory, and performance. This translation of events in the storytelling mode is further subject to another mode of translation, when edited into a film, typically by someone other than the original storyteller. In recounting an event from his life, my uncle Nasser seems to carry the burden of these events and then finds a way—often physical—to release that memory and its weight. Because these movements were best understood over a long period of time, editing between them became difficult and at times traumatic. This installation therefore revisits the original interview, which lasting two hours was the longest conversation my uncle and I had ever had.

Mike Evans and Stephen Foster
The Prince George Métis Elders' Documentary Project

The project video includes a series of interviews and video journeys that depict and document the Métis community of Prince George and BC. There are various video elements from cultural workshops, historical documentation, Métis music, medicine walks, individual and group interviews of local Métis Elders on the Island Cache and the history of Métis in Prince George. These video and audio elements are interlinked with one another to form a non-linear multi-vocal narrative that allows for inclusivity and simultaneity to inform and educate audiences on local Métis history as well as generating compelling and emotive audio and visuals. The simultaneity also creates unique and intriguing juxtapositions and vignettes of content and image. This fragmentation while metaphorically represents the complexity of the contemporary Métis Diaspora it also works to create a deeper more intuitive understanding of the local community, its history, and dynamics.

Fundamentally this project is an artistic exploration and experimentation with the form of documentary and its conceptualization of representation. Audience members can choose material by navigating the screens or by just watching as the video plays through the various sections of the DVD. The way in which different people will activate certain material at differing times will create intertextual inferences between the various screens.
The interactivity embedded in the video elements engages the viewer/audience in a dialogue with the video imagery and content that is beyond mere passive reaction. As the viewer/audience navigates through material, via mouse on screen, they build their own connections and construct their own narratives. Interviews can play off and inform one another or they could combine with imagery of surrounding locations and historical information giving a broader contextualization.

Stephanie Spray
Untitled (bed)

Untitled (bed) is a nine-minute single shot of an ordinary occurrence, that of a child performing household chores—folding laundry and making the bed. While such a nonevent would hardly warrant a footnote in most ethnographies, in the greater schema of analysis and argumentation, this ethnographically inflected, looping video intently focuses on a child's dutiful performance of an everyday task. By yoking itself to its subject in a visual dance, the video calls our attention to the physicality of the ethnographer/videographer, whose relationship to the subject, a Nepali boy, is unclear. The darkened domestic space envelops to initiate an experience that, at times, verges on claustrophobia, and from which details emerge more distinct and poignant—posters and newspapers on the walls, holes in the mosquito net, and the uneven earthen floor. The "exotic" is conjugated with the mundane in the duration of the shot, which exhausts expectations for further character or narrative development.

An abbreviated version of this shot forms a scene in a feature-length nonfiction video, *As Long as There's Breath* (2009), which depicts a Nepali family's struggles for cohesion despite everyday travails and the absence of a beloved son. Extended and isolated from other scenes, *Untitled (bed)* upsets and interrogates a desire for further context or exposition. The subtitles provide the basic narrative thread, as well as an explanation for the boy's activities, but little else is provided to elucidate an otherwise banal act. Instead, the camera lingers over the textures of fabric and the gestures of the boy, whose increasingly hurried work appears both exhaustive and exhausting. Undomesticated and standing alone, this single shot video challenges the viewer to seek meaning through an engagement with the senses, to then reflect and make sense of embodied knowledge.

The video was shot in Lekhnath, Nepal in 2008 and produced in the Sensory Ethnography Laboratory and Film Study Center at Harvard University. Original format DVCPRO–HD. Sound mix by Ernst Karel.

Scott Webel and Jen Webel

House Cats: A Traveling Display of the Museum of Natural & Artificial Ephemerata

Visitors to the Museum of Ephemerata in Austin, Texas, often tell us how meeting our cats is an important part of touring our in-home Dime Museum. The cats greet visitors, do tricks, and model displays. "House Cats" brings our furry co-curators out to meet the world.

The Museum of Natural & Artificial Ephemerata was founded in 1921 by Madame Mercury Curie and Rolls Joyce Jr. The latter was born Rasputin Zaplatynska, great granduncle to Scott Webel, current curator with Jen Webel. This curiosity museum served as a "zoo for endangered species of collection" like collections of saintly relics, Wunderkammern, and dime museums. After being boxed up after the former curators' deaths in the '40s, the Webels reopened the Museum in 1999 out of their house in Tucson, Arizona. Since moving to Austin, Texas, in 2001, the Museum has expanded beyond the original curators' "impermanent collection" to include community thematic shows like "Machines," "Animals," and "Ghosts." These temporary exhibitions are venues for Museum visitors to share cherished objects and their stories with a broader public. During weekly open hours, the costumed curators offer performative tours woven from the narratives of the loaned items and chance events like animal tricks, kombucha tea samples, and explorations of the garden. The project is documented at http://mnae.org.

ETHNOGRAPHIC TERMINALIA:
EXHIBITION REVIEW

Lucian Gomoll, University of California, Santa Cruz

Ethnographic Terminalia is an ongoing, collaborative project that features inventive installations by ethnographers, artists, and individuals who might identify as both. Contributions explore the boundaries of ethnography, challenging traditional disciplinary notions of what we might classify as anthropology or art, and calling into question any such distinctions that might be made during the production or postproduction of an exhibition.

The Ice Box Project Space at Crane Arts in Philadelphia hosted the first iteration of Ethnographic Terminalia. The exhibition was open to the public during the 2009 meeting of the American Anthropological Association (AAA), entitled "The End/s of Anthropology." Curators Craig Campbell, Anabelle Rodriguez, and Fiona McDonald, along with Kate Hennessy and Stephanie Takaragawa, organized the event. They worked with an additional 15 different contributors of 12 installations. Many of the works were shown in previous contexts but were reimagined for Philadelphia in 2009.

The exhibition space was divided into two main rooms, the first featured black walls, called "The Gray Area," and the second featured white walls, called "The Ice Box." The "Media Room," also painted black, was located down the hallway from the first gallery. "The Gray Area" included a mixture of high-tech media installations and low-tech pages of label copy and printed photos. In this dark

Reprinted with permission. Lucian Gomoll. Ethnographic Terminalia. Visual Anthropology Review, Vol. 26, Issue 1, pp. 32–35.

Facing page: general installation view, Philadelphia, 2009.

gallery, visitors encountered various media installations, such as Kate Hennessy and Oliver Neumann's video, "Media on the City: The Lee Building" (Oct 08–Jan 09), which documented the dismantling of a billboard on Vancouver's first skyscraper, and "Unknownterritories" by Roderick Coover, which included an immersive and panoramic photograph from his work within the "Great American Desert." Video installations by Maryam Kashani and Stephanie Spray also illuminated this dark gallery. To the far right of the entrance was Christopher Fletcher's "The Sound of Le Corbusier's Paris." This installation, which Fletcher describes as "an experiment in acousmatic ethnography," invited visitors to stand on block pedestals underneath focused speakers. Here they listened to sounds recorded in or near Le Corbusier's modernist buildings in Paris. The installation challenged us to engage our senses in addition to sight, to explore how the built environment impacts the ways we and others locate ourselves socially, and to do so in Philadelphia.

Fletcher's installation is experimental in nature, as are many of the contributions to Ethnographic Terminalia, and it leaves much open to question and sensorial experience. One consequence of this choice is that his minimal, "not-so-thick" approach requires that visitors bring to the work any prior knowledge they might have of Paris, Le Corbusier, modern architecture, social spaces, and so on. Thus what one comes away with from the installation depends significantly on what one brings to it, which may lead to a variety of interesting as well as undesirable repercussions during postproduction.

Contextually minimalist display techniques are suggestive of how we might interpret an object or a display as "art," as opposed to "artifact." How a display might be framed is critical for understanding a project like Ethnographic Terminalia, which challenges the ways that objects might be categorized or disciplined. Nevertheless, the apparent dialectic between art object and cultural artifact is a problematic fiction of the West but still continues to challenge curators, artists, and ethnographers alike. The works in Ethnographic Terminalia that appear most legible as "contemporary art" include Jayasinhji Jhala's "RannWalk Ocean and Breathings," a dramatic hanging mobile sculpture of found objects, as well as Gordana and Marko Zivkovic's "Lovable Edmonton," a study of Edmonton bus stops that suggested we pay careful attention to mundane sites through the hand-coloring of black-and-white photos. Of course, to call any of these "Art" with a capital A would be seriously reductive; rather, they might be interpreted as such if they are appreciated and contemplated for their formal beauty without much reference to an external context, as is the Western tradition of engaging with art.

Craig Campbell's own contribution to Ethnographic Terminalia, "Mobile Agitational Cinema, Iteration no. 1," was a reimagination of viewing tents used by communist agitators during the 1920s and 1930s. These mobile cinemas attempted to convince indigenous peoples of Siberia to participate in emerging political debates. Rather than screening a film from the period in a contemporary manner, Campbell "made the cut" around the "art/ifact" more broadly, and re-created an entire viewing space. However, Campbell's own twist on this mode of display was not for political persuasion, but rather to "intimate unfamiliar and distant worlds" through slow-moving, close-up images. Thus his mobile cinema installation gestures toward the limits of how we might represent a technology from the early-20th century, when socialist-realist and abstract esthetics performed different social purposes. Campbell himself plays with abstraction, and the installation became surreal when visitors from the Western hemisphere engaged with the images and spatial construction.

Installed on the wall next to Campbell's tent was Mike Evans and Stephen Foster's "The Prince George Me´tis Elders' Documentary Project." This interactive video installation invited visitors to explore visual documents of the Me´tis community of Prince George and British Columbia in Canada. Also in close proximity, and directly across from Campbell's mobile cinema, was Trudi Smith's "Portable Camera Obscura," another fully assembled tent in the large white gallery space. First shown in the Waterton Lakes National Park in Alberta during summer 2009, participants were able to enter the tent to see an actual landscape projected onto an interior wall of the structure. In Crane Arts, however, a painted scene replaced the open-air landscape that was projected onto the interior wall. Smith's contribution was one of the most formally interesting of the exhibition, as it reimagined a very old technology of looking, commonly studied by art historians who are interested in how threedimensional scenarios were once translated into twodimensional schemas. In open-air contexts, Smith's room-sized "camera" functioned as a tool for local communities to explore their relationships to the natural environment. In Crane Arts, however, the installation became one that represented such community organizing, while it sparked other kinds of conversations, often about the technology itself. In addition, the portable camera obscura harkened back to modes of exhibition that relied on alternative viewing tools to engage with objects in a collection.

Examples of displays that incorporated special viewing tools include the Early Modern European cabinets of curiosities (kunstkammern), as well as the 19th century American dime museums. While the former catered to aristocratic audiences, the latter were considered to be "low-brow." Both were similar in how they articulated objects according to different spatial logics when compared with the rationalist, serial mode we are familiar with today. Unlike contemporary mainstream museums, the older examples did not separate art from artifact, myth from "fact," and so on. Rather, the organizational strategies were visually nonhierarchical and mosaic in their suggestion of the variety of relationships between the materials on display. Such "museums" encouraged visitors to engage the objects not only with naked eyes, but also with viewing tools like magnifying glasses. An attention to the conceptual similarities between pre- or anti-disciplinary models of exhibition and Ethnographic Terminalia reveals some of the contemporary exhibition's most interesting and performative dimensions.

A direct reference to the cabinets of curiosities and dime museums was Scott Webel and Jen Webel's "House Cats: A Traveling Display of the Museum of Natural & Artificial Ephemerata." The Webels are curators of an "in-home dime museum," one of the few remaining sites of its kind after the famous closures of Baltimore's American Dime Museum and New York's Freakatorium. For Ethnographic Terminalia, the Webels presented a curious display of a cat whose belly would rise as if it were breathing. Because the cat's body looked eerily real, one might inquire as to whether or not it was an altered taxidermy specimen. Indeed, today's media focus on "reality" might prompt visitors to be preoccupied with determining which parts of the display were "real" and which were not. But such issues do not seem to concern the Webels. Instead, they frame their work as in conversation with wunderkammern and dime museums, as performative "ephemera."

Regardless of intentions, confusing or unclear displays like "House Cats" will prompt viewers to ask questions, questions that are beyond the control of the exhibitors' vision, which we might consider to be a mixed blessing. In the 19th century, framing objects as questionable in dime museums simultaneously undermined the authority claimed by state-funded institutions while reifying various hegemonies pertaining to the perceived social and natural order. Often audience projections reflected ideas about biological determinism and non-Western cultures. Indeed, Franz Boas cited such misguided interpretations as the reason for his retreat from public anthropology in the early 1900s (Hinsley 1991:363). Today, these kinds of displays come already equipped with a problematic social interactivity that is at once alarming in that they still provoke socially irresponsible responses like racism and sexism, or enabling questions of "authenticity" and also radical as they undermine any absolute authority that could be claimed by those who curate or produce a work.

Erica Lehrer and Hannah Smotrich's installation invites participation from visitors by encouraging them to place images of Jewishness into the two categories of "OK" and "Not OK," and asking them to explain their choices by writing on the wall. As with any display that mobilizes its contents on open-ended terms rather than with authoritative foreclosures, "Jewish? Heritage? In Poland?" frames postproduction as an integral part of the installation. It encouraged participants to consider the complexities of cultural representation and to take responsibility for their actions. Responses written in the designated spaces ranged from insulting to remarkable, such as "you constrained me to two unacceptable choices. I was going to opt out until I saw that someone put them all on 'OK'" and the succinct exclamation, "I demand more options!"

Indeed, the questions provoked by alternative display methods are echoed in the main text to Ethnographic Terminalia: "Has this work been edited or is it presented as raw data? What is participant observation anyway? What constitutes witnessing? What is the role of the spectator in all of this?" (Campbell et al. 2009). Even if a visitor walked past the introductory labels without reading, similar questions were sure to emerge. How someone might respond to such questions, however, is not predictable. One would hope that the decisions made during the exhibition's production would encourage questions that are self-aware and critical, and would resonate thoughtfully beyond the immediate spatiotemporal environment. Thinking of the AAA's conference theme "The End/s of Anthropology," Ethnographic Terminalia was successful as a conversation with the conference participants. The exhibition contributors approached the title's double entendre, "end/s," as both purpose and limits, from a variety of interesting perspectives.

For the most part, Ethnographic Terminalia relied on a serial spatial order that is conventional to art galleries. In the future, the curators might explore the performative and critical potential of looking at alternative histories of exhibition and spatial articulation, for the possibilities that such examples could offer the curators' post- or anti-disciplinary goals.

Indeed, a constriction imposed by Ethnographic Terminalia's own boundaries seemed to be the gallery context itself, for some of the installations. For example, while many of the displays were performative and produced a desire to learn more about the content of each work, a noticeable limitation, or "end" if I may, was a lack of significantly "thick" explanations to accompany some of the works. I suspect this was a deliberate choice on the part of the organizers to avoid what we may call "label fatigue," or overwhelming the audience with too much information about 12 installations. In truth, it is a problem to which this author cannot offer an unproblematic solution. Additionally, some of the installations might have been more "effective" in their open-air contexts, such as "Portable Camera Obscura," which Smith claims successfully mobilized local communities in Alberta. Similarly, visitors to Lehrer and Smotrich's installation might have vastly different investments in how they relate to Jewish representation in Philadelphia when compared with the initial staging of the work in Krakow, Poland. A comparative study of reactions to their project would be interesting indeed. Ethnographic Terminalia will follow the AAA to New Orleans in 2010. Documentation from the exhibit may be viewed at http://www.ethnographicterminalia.org.

References

Campbell, Craig, Fiona McDonald, and Anabelle Rodriguez
    2009   Ethnographic Terminalia Label Copy. Posted in "The Gray Area"
              gallery of Crane Arts, Philadelphia, PA.

Hinsley, Curtis M.
    1991   The World as Marketplace: Commodification of the Exotic at
              the World's Columbian Exposition, Chicago, 1893. In Exhibiting
              Cultures: The Poetics and Politics of Museum Display. Ivan
              Karp and Steven D. Lavine, eds. Pp. 344–365. Washington, DC:
              Smithsonian Institution Press.

www.ingramcontent.com/pod-product-compliance
Lightning Source LLC
Chambersburg PA
CBHW040138270326
41927CB00020B/3441